FINISHING LINE PRESS
www.finishinglinepress.com

The Coffin Makers

poems by

Heather Corbally Bryant

Finishing Line Press
Georgetown, Kentucky

The Coffin Makers

ISBN 979-8-88838-139-7 First Edition

ACKNOWLEDGMENTS

"Sitting Out the Solstice Under the Japanese Maple Tree" was previously published in *REFUGE*, Ed., Susan Edwards Richmond, Pen and Anvil Press, September 2020.

Publisher: Leah Huete de Maines
Editor: Christen Kincaid
Cover Art: Edna St Vincent Millay Statue
Author Photo: Richard Howard, Richard Howard Photography, www.richardhowardphotography.com

Cover Design: Elizabeth Maines McCleavy

Order online: www.finishinglinepress.com
also available on amazon.com

Author inquiries and mail orders:
Finishing Line Press
P. O. Box 1626
Georgetown, Kentucky 40324
U. S. A.

Table of Contents

For my students—past, present, and future,
and for my colleagues

Crocus

One purple bloom amidst leftover brown leaves—no
Reason to believe, having lived life in fear—we

Can remember why we are here—

To begin—a virus spreads in our computers, then
In our communities—how do I learn to be free

After a lifetime of imprisonment—

How do I begin to believe again—one purple
Crocus sprouts amidst spring leaves, tossed by wind,

My son calls from India—

Hyderabad, I believe, my children
Scattered like the leaves—here now, the virus begins—one

First crocus bloom, on one of the last days of

February—mid-winter changing seasons.

The Light This March

We debate the Farmer's Almanac—the light this
March falls soft and warm, spring appears early—turning
House hunters out before April,

Ahead of schedule—the familiar comes upon us—more
Crocus shoots sprout—to begin at the beginning—
I stretch my arms wide—my son boards a plane to

Return from India passing through Dubai, where they
Will take all disembarking passengers' temperatures—
Peculiar, this world we've created where anyone

Can hop a plane to anywhere in the world—by
Virtue of having gone everywhere, we may
Soon learn we can go nowhere—

This Morning the Geese Are Flying Home

Perambulating through our neighborhood this morning, the dog
Points, as her breed has taught her to do—she nudges her paw
Skyward with equipoise—my eye follows, traveling upwards—

Towards a gaggle of geese flying home, two days after we
Have turned the clocks ahead—a gaggle of geese heads back
Northeast from southern climes—they tuck their wings into a

Geometric V, flapping all the way, the pup's fur flies up,
Bristling in fear as she does with any unfamiliarity—fear
Runs deep in both of us—we've each been trained to be

Wary of the unknown, to be circumspect in our evaluations—
It is unclear to me where her trauma resides, all I do know is
She was born by a roadside in Tennessee—rounding the

Corner, I see the natural order prevails, asserting itself—geese
Forming a V, heading for a reservoir down the street.

Social Distancing

Now that we crisscrossed the world, we have to untangle
The wires we bound ourselves together with—as COVID-19
Spreads around us, accelerated by our ceaseless

Circumnavigating of the globe—case by case pops up—we
Have to think about how we will live in other ways—perhaps
The universe is sending us a message of mindfulness—

How will we be mindful of our new practices: social
Distancing, quarantines, elbow bumps, standing six feet
Away in an attempt to slow the spread, flatten the curve—

The forsythia hasn't bloomed yet—maybe when we can
Begin to see familiar yellow blossoms we can
Go about our merry ways again—

But today, for the first time, the WHO declared a pandemic.

Shedding

It could be anywhere—floating through air, we look out
Our curtain bare windows at night—the world quiets,
Flattens, darkens—when I go to sleep in late evening, I

Do not hear the freight trains rushing—it feels as though
Life itself has stopped—all we do to feel human and alive
Has been put on hold—that is all we can do to stop this

Brand new virus floating into our lives—it appears lethal,
Virulent, mysterious—to spread without intent—we dread
What may happen next as the numbers multiply

Exponentially—we are all scared, most of all, we fear
What we do not know—after all, the virus could be anywhere.

A Giant Pumpkin Rolling Down the Street

Magnifications of the virus appear many times over
On our screens—yellow and orange-red blobs edged
With dark rims, appearing sinister, malevolent, like dots

Under a microscope gone wrong—we fear what we
Do not know—so we close everything—we peer at
Strangers, scrutinizing them for any signs of disease—

A cough, a sneeze, something to indicate they are
Unwell, anything to suggest we should avoid them—like
Animals in herds, we avoid other humans in distress—

The virus even appears in my dreams—a giant pumpkin of
Sickliness rolling down the street, coming after me.

Early Observations: A Record

i

Grocery stores emptied of bottled water, toilet paper, and hand sanitizer.

ii

The midnight train heading down the tracks, departing the Framingham Depot for points west is silent.

iii

Fewer planes cross the skies; their jet trails leave fainter marks.

iv

Traffic almost ceases—rush hour virtually disappears as wfh becomes standard practice for those of us lucky enough not to be deemed essential.

v

We spend more time in nature; we cook elaborate meals; the dog is pleased that we never leave her alone.

vi

My anxiety rises; I know it is one of the hallmarks of being alive.

vii

I am in the high-risk population—those of us over a certain age—these days feel eerie, like the weeks after the towers came tumbling down.

Flattening the Curve

My father once gave me an early map from London to Land's End—earth
Crinkles, wrinkled, in bands of latitudes to take us there—

We speak, these days, of flattening the curve, of social distancing—
Anything to prevent a surge of this virus we do not yet understand—

These times challenge us to turn inward, to work backwards, leaning
On our inner resources—the social order as we know it has been

Upended—we learn drops from one person can be spread to another—perhaps
It can live in the air suspended—words float through my mind—

A pandemic thrust into our midst—and how do we begin to count our
Days in new ways—when all distractions fade away and we are left

Only with our essential selves, with what is pure, distinct, distilled—what
Has been whipped, stilled, spun like sugar, cotton candy

Strands of molten glass cascading down into icicles and castles; the only
Way we can see where we are is to stop, and pull out a paper map.

At the Grocery Store, Early Quarantine

i

We have been told to stay a safe distance from other people—six feet at the minimum.

ii

Strangers peer at one another, then look away—evaluating the risk, per se.

iii

We have been reminded not to touch door knobs, or handles, or grocery carts with our bare hands.

iv

Some people wear gloves—most paper products have vanished
from the shelves—signs limiting us to two items

v

Preside over empty aisles—in our minds, we have vanished, differences not erased, but instead magnified.

vi

As we look around, we calculate our chances of staying alive.

Unintended Consequences, Easter

I

We take a long walk in late afternoon—people are out strolling,
Perambulating—the elderly, hunched forward, walking with

Care, taking notice of where they put their feet—dogs straining
On leashes—a spaniel tugging his owner along—a young couple

Holding hands in the mid-March sunshine, pushing a baby
Carriage with checkered cloths enveloping their new infant—

Routines altered, interrupted as we seek to find our footing in
This unfamiliar landscape—I think of Yeats's words from more

Than a century ago—also at Easter—"all changed, changed utterly"
From what we used to know, just a few weeks ago.

II

It is fashionable, these days, to speak of unintended consequences—
Of seeing the errors of our ways, of the butterfly effect—now that

We have brought the world together, we have to take it apart,
Piece by piece—the specks of dust from the African desert

Can make their way across several oceans and continents to
Seed an invasive species all around the universe—the rotors of

Motor boats carry water lilies that can clog whole ponds—
Cleaving to what was once there—and in our midst the virus

Settles in—best case scenarios say we can flatten the curve.

Notes From the Plague

i

We speak now of the before, *before* we say, in hushed notes, nodding.

ii

We no longer venture into stores, to the degree possible we order online— The RO rate for this virus is believed to be two to three, a high ratio.

iii

Californians have been ordered to shelter in place, an entire state full of people not allowed to leave their homes.

iv

Fear courses through all of us as the numbers race ahead—we are in a race we do not want to win.

v

My friend and her family was evacuated from Chile in the middle of the night, flying from Santiago to Bogotá to Kennedy airport with their belongings.

vi

The map of where we can go compresses, until we can hold it in one hand.

vii

My daughter speaks of her loneliness until her fiancé can get there—we laugh about the possibility that a fish might be able to keep her company.

viii

Each of us is cast back on our own souls as we distance, watching the numbers climb.

ix

The before will now no longer be recognizable to any one of us.

The Red Virus

I wish I hadn't seen the picture, the image of
Black and white pock-marked lungs,
Riddled with holes, like craters on the moon—

As we learned how to go to the moon, we forgot
About taking care of one another—we neglected
The essentials—and now, because of our

Foolish short-sightedness, we have endangered
The entire human race—how do we tell the
Dancer from the dance? We are all stuck in our

Homes, or apartments, those of us fortunate
Enough to have them, but meanwhile the red
Coronavirus chases us down the streets—

Red blobs stuck on a circular crown, like a
Ring of cloves on a roast—a chef in a white
Hat serving an entire restaurant empty of

Guests—in London no weddings can have
More than five celebrants—in a world gone
Mad it is difficult to forget what we have

Seen, it is difficult to close our eyes at night.

Boston, Shelter in Place, First Full Day

Quiet streets, people walking with blue masks poking out of
Their pockets, or wrapped around their fingers—saucer
Magnolia buds peeking white against a translucent sky—

These late days of March, we are all afraid—as the red
Virus gallops along, coming down the streets for us—family
Groups walking, social distancing is the new

Most common phrase—people now walk six feet apart,
Shutters pulled, blinds yanked down—the world has gone
Into retreat—

I will wait for the cherry magnolias to come into full bloom.

Prayers for the Pandemic

i

Now we say it is a pandemic and the United States has more cases than any other country in the world.

ii

Numbers of cases rise faster than the sea levels nearing the skies.

iii

I alternate between panic and concentration; people clear out all the clutter from their houses; dumpsters are hard to come by these days.

iv

Many others bake bread, their hands kneading air pockets; yeast is difficult to find at the grocery store.

v

It is impossible to see with the naked eye, the virus deadly, invisible, also dead; apparently, a dead virus is much more difficult to kill than a live one.

vi

In one week, the United States has gone from 18,200 cases to 85,498, as of the news this morning.

vii

These clusters have migrated from bats to livestock in a Chinese market, so one theory goes—now it is circling the entire globe.

viii

World without end, please hear my prayer, spare us from ever more suffering.

Northern Vernal Equinox

Forsythia branches sprout egg-yolk yellow overnight—
They spring into full bloom, like summer blossoms,
Like forest fairies, harbingers of spring, far from
Suffering—

Earth smells warm again, warm and full of feast—earth
Tips southward towards the meridian—all things
Will be made new again—infection fears spark
From the prospect

Of bodies piled high outside morgues—people turned
To stone by disease—refrigeration trucks appear,
Makeshift morgues arrive to store the bodies dying
Too quickly

For us to begin to count accurately; a mortician explains
Humans need to be able to say good-bye; iPads are
Propped against windows—the last embrace
Substituted by a wave and a scream—

Every evening, New Yorkers bang pots and pans to honor the
Laborers doing the impossible work of the saving.

Pink Moon

Our first night here coincides with the night of a full moon—
I walk out to the woodshed to fetch logs for our first fire—

A huge moon rises behind the clearing, pink and shining—
The moon in perigee—syzygy, closest to earth—named
After phlox the flower—egg moon, sprouting grass moon,

Hare moon, fish moon, still glinting through trees at sunrise.

The Red Fox

Perhaps this fox will be our spirit animal—he
Scampered through my dreams, leading

Me to this oasis here on earth—much that I
Dreamed of is to be found here, among

Worn thin graves climbing through new green
Grass—at last I feel at home—a hearth,

Dream, home—I have been on a quest for the
Last decade trying to find a place I belong—

May it be here, may it be a home—I suppose you
Could say the red fox called us back here.

Good Friday Walk, Ossipee

What to pray for—Christ on the cross all afternoon, a miserable
Rainy, sleety day in Ossipee—

All in an honest day's work, world turned upside down, God
Nowhere to be found—

A field hospital in Central Park—extra funeral directors on call—
Refrigeration trucks lined up to receive

The bodies—the world has gone topsy turvy on us—city
Convention centers turned into a hospital,

National Guard troops on patrol, marching up and down the
Sidewalks, rifles slung over their backs—but,

In this case, there is nothing visible to attack.

Hydrangeas at Twilight, I

Fluffy dried sepia blossoms sway in the wind, sky
Darkens midnight blue behind, shards of indigo—

Behind the red barn, below the steep hillside, like a
Sentry guarding this old land, here for centuries—

Ages and ages, a stone hut at the bottom of our
Driveway—something peaceable comes in

Knowing how long humans have inhabited this
Stretch of earth—Venus rises, once bloomed

Hydrangeas cast shadows—a few gum drop
Petals fall, floating, twirling to the ground.

The Red Zone

It is international Holocaust Survivor Day—those
Who remain worry they won't be able to speak their

Truths—the horrors they witnessed—humans have
Remarkably short memories—the liminal spaces now

Take precedence—the red zone barring the threshold
From here to here—making us safe—pink clouds

Descend at twilight—radiologists act as translators,
Ordinary citizens step up to do whatever they can—

The pope has issued a papal interdict—there can be
No sacraments performed during this time of crisis—

No sacraments in a pandemic—the stories of goodness
Triumphing, buried beneath our gaze—those are

The places where we must first turn our attention.

Covid Blues

Sing a song of the pandemic blues—what will our days look
Like afterwards—we speak to each other in a daze—what will

This hazy future appear to be afterwards—will we curl inwards,
Crumpled up into fetal balls or, will we rush back, arms outstretched

Into the lives we used to know? We speak as futurists must have
Once predicted—imagine a world without movies, or restaurants,

Or shops, or any distractions familiar to use—we are like beings
Wondering what might happen if we could fly—except, now we

Did fly—and hundreds of thousands are dying in the aftermath.

Wood Stack: A Mouse and Her Babies

A mouse just gave birth in the logs stacked beside our fire pit—April
Birthdays for six tiny squirming, warming creatures—

My son and I dislodge them with care, setting them underneath
A ring of pine trees, by the rocks scattered on our hillside—we tiptoe

Away, afraid—meanwhile, the mother scampers up and down
Searching for her babies, frantic—late in the day we reunite

Them, bringing soft pine needles to the nest she had created—we
Hope she will care for them after we have tiptoed away—

We've heard it said that, once human hands touch their babies,
Their mouse mothers no longer want them.

A Riddle

If there was one reported case of COVID-19 in New York
On the first of March, that means there were thousands of
Ill people wandering around the city circulating the virus

Every which way—the virus was arriving by the plane load
From Europe in late winter—human beings are terrible at
Understanding the exponential function of risk—our minds

Cannot venture there; as the riddle goes, if a pond is fully
Covered with lily pads, when would the pads cover half of
The pond—day thirty-nine—it only takes one day more for

Numbers to go high enough to choke the pond so hard that it can
Barely breathe, barely host our lives—so our lungs strive
To survive—as it turns out, like the ponds, humans are

Proving to be exceptionally good hosts of this novel virus.

Chickville Corner Church, Circa 1857

New graves stuck with artificial flowers, covered over
Dirt, newly disturbed—

Two men conversing on a cloudy Sunday afternoon—
One hundred thousand

More body bags have been ordered so far, more people
In the United States

Have died in this pandemic than were killed in Vietnam—
The numbers climb—

Here earth appears sweet and kind, gentle mounds of
Grieving and believing—

Tethered in faith—meanwhile in the outside world we
Appear to be losing

Our sense of grace—I want to behold and to hold—all
Life spread out, divinely

On a grassy corner, bordering two roads where I have
Retreated from

The frenzy of the known world—sun breaks through
Crackled glass windows,

Bubbled with wear, weather, and age.

In Memoriam, Eavan Boland, April 2020

I was looking out at April leafy snowflakes falling
On the green pear tree sprouts when news of her

Sudden death in Dublin reached me—she was the
First poet I heard put woman and poet in the same

Breath—daring to say the unspeakable, breathing
Difficult life into the unimaginable, part of my

Pantheon of imaginative sprites who guide me away
From darkness, towards light—I read her poem,

"First Year" in *The New Yorker*—the one where she asks
Where does the soul of a marriage reside?

After, I read everything else I could—her poems
Accompanied me through years of birthing, nursing,

Writing by circles of lamplight after midnight—she
Guided me through the crevices of alphabets and

Landscapes, known and unknown; I would imagine
Her writing alone in her suburban Dublin aerie—

Putting down the words as fast as she could—in the
Midst of April flakes falling fast.

Evensong

Rounding hills surround me, the hills of Ossipee—uneven
Peaks dipping, rising, undulating, smoothing—

Apricot tinges into indigo; velvet purple twilight
Fingers—my daughter may marry at a faraway

Courthouse—I don't think I will be able to travel
By then—let evening come, evensong, midnight

Blue descends—a rocket from China detaches,
Perhaps scattering parts to New York City and

Beyond—the afterbirth wouldn't detach after twin
B, my daughter, was born—I almost bled out, a

Phrase whose meaning I did not know until that noon—the
Pandemic rages taking so much with it—

Where we begin again; the comfort of humans
In a stone church warmed by sunshine—

When I look up, skies have gone dark, bumpy
Hills still holding speckles of sunshine—

Let the evening come.

Memorial Day

Air hangs heavy this Memorial Day, epidemiologists
Now say virus droplets can spread over six feet away—

Disruptions abound—hundreds of thousands have lost
Lives, loved ones, sanity, savings, houses, livelihoods—

My daughter asks me to look for her birth certificate
So she can marry at a courthouse—a year ago all three

Of my children came home—now I long to put my arms
Around them, tuck them in safely at night—I think of

Her, young and brave, standing before a judge to say *I*
Do, I long to be there, to hold her, to say everything will

Be OK, but those days are so very far away for all of us.

America, on Fire

i

A Black man slips a counterfeit bill on a counter
In Minneapolis—

The police are called—hatred reigns and he is
Kneed to the ground, a policeman's foot

Holding down his neck—pretty soon, he
Cannot breathe—another Black life gone.

ii

But this time headlines hold for more than a hot
Minute—they capture more than a nanosecond

Of our feeble attentions—America
Is broken.

This summer the fires are heating up—we've
All been stuck inside

iii

Losing our jobs, our hearts, our minds—we're
Beyond fairness here—

Basic dignities denied, rich people
Fleeing to the countryside—

A breath, a job, a doctor, a place to live—are
These such impossible requests?

iv

Protests spread east and west, outward from
The center until they reach the coasts—

The President tweets hate, rage, vitriol—inciting
A desperate desire for violence

While he retreats to his villa in Florida where he
Golfs among palm trees.

v

Counting his riches like King Midas, only worse—nobody
Can mind the store anymore—

We have lost our grip on reality—what would my
Father say if he were here?

We can no longer have no fear—violence defines our
Lives, reaches beyond our grasp.

vi

Police cars overturned, burned, protesters shot
With rubber bullets and worse—one headline

vii

Misspelled the murdered man's name.

Say Their Names

Say their names the placards read; say their names
We chant again, never to be forgotten—

When does the forgetting begin?
Are we each an island unto ourselves?

Where do we jump in to swim? Where do we swim
Where we have never been before—

The conversation already elusive, and yet she
Persisted—power spills onto the streets—

Where do we turn for the release?

The Abandoned Tennis Court

Old walls, stones piled high from decades, even
Centuries of use—an enclosed clay court, weeds
Growing down along where the net should have

Been—a wooden bench alongside the wall, perhaps
For spectators, an umpire, or elderly players to rest
In the midst of a forest—

Edges blend into grass—gate swung open, I can
Smell summer oldness, years of playing, strawberries
Ripening nearby pine trees—

A glade, above a diamond-paned window and a meadow—a
Place to feel safe, perhaps, safe from whatever is to
Come—

Red geraniums overflowing window boxes, rocking chairs
Set out on the porch—I long for the feeling of safety,

The one I associate with arriving and departing, the space
Hanging between the two—I tiptoe across the surface

Where one faint line peaks through the leaves, summer after
Summer of habit, and perhaps happiness.

For My Daughter Being Married by a Judge in Omaha

A bouquet of white lilies, sweetheart pink roses, a hint of blush
On your day that is not turning out at all how we thought it

Would—delivered just in time by an Omaha florist—the day
You two tie the knot, my hope for you is that you do not have

To let go of any of your hopes—may he always be good to you,
May you be good to him; marriage is a peculiar institution—

On this first day past the solstice, may you find love, redress,
The color of happiness as we learn to live in this altered world,

The one where are all the ordinary rules have been broken—when
I see you walk into the courtroom, tears stream through my

Zoom screen—it's hard to tell your expression through your
Mask—it looks hot there—a long way from Boston and the blizzard

You arrived in—it was also snowing the day I brought you home,
You in your soft yellow cap, the color of a chick's fluff, the one

I lost in one of our many moves—we can't hold onto time, but may it
Hold you in its arms, just as today you clutch your fluttering bouquet.

Black Bear, Nightfall

At first, he was just a black shape slipping along at twilight—across
The periphery of my eye, chasing a wilderness corridor,

Until he came into focus, stopped, and turned towards me and
The dog, now staring back at us, right below the deck—

He appeared mesmerized by us—the pup began barking as if
To alert me a bit late, danger—

I have not seen one of these creatures before; he stood so still
Before he slipped into shadowed wood, disappearing from this

Clearing—he turned to look back one more time as if to make sure
He had seen us, that we were as he thought we were—

After he left, we looked back at where he had been and it was
Impossible to believe he had been there, that he was not

Simply a mirage, after all.

Sitting Out the Solstice Under a Japanese Maple Tree

Sitting beneath green feathered leaves
with their cutout shapes—

Underneath a canopy of grace—a cooling welcome
today when it's ninety degrees in the shade,

The experience of being—the sign out front says
Black Lives Matter today, now, always—

Beside slow turtle crossing, children playing,
the places we drive by—

Both haunted and tainted by our lives—we could
spend a lifetime redoing everything—

Feathered green leaves casting dappled shadows
on my bare white legs sitting beside

The farm stand selling garlic scapes, strawberry,
and kale—where do we plant our shoots

And cuttings—it is the beginning of grace to
retrace our roots—though we can never

Recoup the shootings, the lies, the violence—
beneath their canopy of desire, flying on

The wings of hope and deed, we can learn from
this new beginning, breathing the grace

Of longing and belonging, we can only start again
from where we are just now.

Planting Perennial Splits Late in June

We plant the last of my friend's splits on this first morning
After my daughter's faraway wedding in this time of strangeness
Abiding—

It was perhaps strangest at the beginning when we had to keep
Figuring out how to live in this year when the virus
Rages free—

We plant hostas, columbine, delphinium, white border sedum that won last
Season's horticultural prize—

We see how one plant can cleave to the next beside the roots of happiness—and
How I wish for her an entire garden free of weeds.

Soon after My Children's Leaving

It began to rain soon after my children left—
Perhaps matching my mood in a 21st century
Recreation of Ruskin's
Pathetic Fallacy—
Nothing can match our late afternoon July
Swims at Little Dan Hole Pond—
We debate the dilemmas of existence—I
Do my best to hold back my cries; this
Saying good-bye is
Never easy—
Especially in the midst of a global pandemic
When everything is more fraught—you three
Who have driven most of the way across the
Country so we could see each other in
Safety—
I think of you now, travelling west on the
Massachusetts Turnpike—
I hold the tears back, they are no help to
Anyone right now—deep cool drizzle
Begins to spatter on the driveway—it
Was ninety degrees much of the time you
Were here—and now just as you are
Leaving, the weather will be breaking.

The Sourwood Tree

The first time I drive by my old house, on the
Eponymously named Home Avenue,

I do a double take—something is different—but
I cannot say what—the façade looks stark

Naked, open, exposed—it has not been repainted
Or enlarged, just has had new windows

Added—more than a cosmetic necessity—and then
I realize, it's the old sourwood tree that's gone, cut

Down, chopped, eliminated—the tree sprouted soft
Yellow blossoms in autumn, vermilion leaves—it

Gave recollection and desire, shade—it once had a
Birdfeeder installed to provide entertainment—

Now it's all gone, all of it, memories known only to me.

Virus, Summer

What we are debating this summer: the true cost of a human life,
Black, white, or whatever color we can come up with—

Cops shoot at protesters for no probable cause or worse,
We swaddle one another—

The RO rates climb; we have to expect every community's
Infection rate to be at least five percent, at best—

Did you hear, college towns will become the new cruise ships?
Thousands of human beings sharing the same air conditioning;

One at a time, we will perhaps stand in line for food—we are
Better off to sit inside awaiting relief—this virus is unseen—

Spreading its way into our eyes, our nostrils, even as we sleep.

White Hydrangeas at Twilight, II

Luminescent at twilight, white hydrangeas bloom, blossom, like
Monet's Japanese lanterns scatted around his Giverny garden—

Bulbs of yellow magic, pale orbs of midnight in sunshine—the
Light of summer, August, fireflies, of dancing with our

Eyes open running headlong into dusk where mosquitoes hover, drowsy waiting
To pounce; high in our skies, the NEOWISE Comet prepares to
Fly.

Hurricane Isaias

Hurricane Isaias crashing up the coast—
Tomorrow, it may turn inland

Scattering a tornado or two—human
Beings are not particularly

Good at changing plans, or, apparently,
At uncertainty—

We are lost without the idea of
Familiarity—school starts in the fall—

But now, we cannot say that with
Any clarity—to follow the guidelines

Assiduously would mean football fields
The shape of classrooms, masks

Hiding how our mouths move—the loss
Of what amounts to any approximation of

Normalcy while we wait for a vaccine—until
The vaccine, until people believe that to

Be inoculated is a necessity.

Notice This Present Moment

Notice this present moment—brook running beside us,
Fingernail moon stretched above, a white cuticle in clear
Sky,

Indigo dimming to twilight—road curves right, following a
Retaining wall's bend, sloping against an embankment—

This August sky, this late summer evensong, dusk to
Birds swimming along, we are well past the last of mid-summer—

Peace comes in knowing what is past can no longer do
Harm—nor can borrowing from future stories be helpful—

Notice only this present moment, skin touching air, windows rolled
Down, songs blaring on the old-fashioned radio.

The King's Psalms

Beneath the floor boards of a fourteenth-century manor in England,
An archeological digger unearthed a packrat's nest filled with torn

Scraps of illuminated manuscripts, preserved for six centuries—beneath this
Wooden parquet floor, dug up for repairs, builders

Discovered areas of interest, not for building but for learning—specks of
Gold around the edges, monks' calligraphy intact, just as it had been,

Taken to a safe place to be examined, when scholars began to piece the precious
Scraps back together—at once, they discovered a second single extant

Copy of the King's Psalms.

Moon Time

Full moon over Ossipee mountains—glimpsed at 3:45 am,
Moonshine, moon shadow, moon glow over long-stretched

Lawn, Milky Way constellations arriving on September's wing—rings
Of light, circles of planets orbiting—if we are lucky,

We may catch one last shooting star.

To the Woman Standing Outside TD Bank

We tuck these stories away in privacy, where no one can
See them—

Domestic violence is up over three hundred percent
Since the start of the pandemic—

The least safe place for a woman is at home—a sign
At the dentist's office reads: *Do you feel safe at home?*

The woman was shot by her husband while she was waiting
For the doors of the bank where she worked to open—

Five more minutes and she could have stayed alive; she was
Seeking safety, instead, she ensured only that there were witnesses.

North Complex Fire, Plume

By now over five million acres have burned, spreading across
Many landscapes, scorching earth apace—tens of thousands of

People have fled their homes, red and orange plumes flare on
Hectares of scarred, damaged lands—did the fire burn everyone's

Lungs? All vegetation was destroyed, leaving every timber
Exposed to catch fire at the instant of concatenation—

On the opposite coast, Hurricane Sally arrives, making
Landfall with a dramatic crush of waves—how can the west

Be saved? The hoses are not long enough to reach the inferno.

A Bowl of Apples Sitting on the Kitchen Counter

i

A bowl of McIntosh and Cortland apples sits on the counter—shapes of grapes
Baked into the ceramic edge—

ii

Twin gods of fire and water lap at our perimeters—some say, but perhaps they
Always have, that the end is near.

iii
Apples picked from orchards on a dappled muggy Sunday.

iv

A bowl of red and green apples stacked on the kitchen
Counter on an ordinary Friday in the middle of September—

v

We are nearing the autumnal equinox.

vi

I hold one round apple in my hand, contemplating its sweetness.

The Coffin Makers

I imagine the coffins—the coffin makers must be keeping
Busy these days—business must be good—funeral directors

Too, with all the arrangements they must be making—the toll
This death count is taking—each of these dots represents

A life lost to COVID-19, a virus in the extreme—seven months
And counting into a full-fledged pandemic on a scale not

Seen for a century—some say we were due—a red vase of
Carnations, deep red, crimson, steadies me as I witness

This suffering in what we now call this unprecedented season.

Time Out of Mind

We call this time unprecedented because we have no other
Words for it—no other time—time out of mind—our lives,

Our bank accounts, our families, our jobs disrupted, tossed
Up in the air everywhere—

It is raining this morning when I read of the death of Derek
Mahon, another figure who seemed immortal; he joins

Seamus Heaney in the unknown world, having been given
His time to die, his words eloquent at the beginning of this

Peculiar time, a time stretching beyond any of the words we
Might have invented for it.

And the World Went Away

Last March, the world adjacent to us vanished with
Safety tape, orange signs announcing the closure of

All the places, planes stopped flying, trains stayed
In their stations, buses were left in unheated depots—

Movie theater parking lots emptied—the virus drove
Us all inside to wait until the danger of contamination

Passed—but, then, in an instant, summer came—days
Grew long again, we went outside in search

Of sunlight and desire, ice cream and carousels—
Leafy hot days, cooling pools in the shade—we

Couldn't wait anymore until one wave tossed into
The next—now the threat of contagion has

Surpassed our deepest fears for the coming winter.

Not Another Ice Age

We were supposed to be entering another ice age, or so the science teacher
Says, she turns back to me, and says this through her mask on an indigo

October day—and yet, and yet, instead, the days are warmer than they have
Ever been this autumn, everything is happening a month earlier than
Expected—

Acorns toppled underfoot—walking on them is like rolling our toes through
A forest, a backrub manqué is here to stay—here today,

Now, always the consensus seems to be the foliage has already peaked—reds
Are muted into a subdued disarray—these October days come inside us—

I want to take them and hold them inside me, looking for the path's
Next turn amidst this pine-needled forest, leftover from the first glacial retreat.

These October Afternoons

On these October afternoons, the road turns far ahead of me—a dirt path
Winding, brooks gushing over ledge when we ask, when did it rain this hard?

As if we were not looking all summer long—ferns browning, feathering
Against stone walls, perhaps the remains of an early saw mill—we are here,

Along for the ride—I miss my mom in this soft light; she said October was
Her favorite month because the month brought her me, her only child; she always

Bought me chrysanthemums—we celebrated my birthday together when she
Had already entered hospice—in the end, she and I were alone together when her

Death came—I hope I comforted her; I did my best.
Silver buckets attached to sugar maples, tapping for syrup's gold—it's odd, even

Seven years later, when your mother can no longer wish you a happy birthday.

Unprecedented

We talk of unprecedented—as in without precedent—not
Ever having occurred before, at least in recent centuries.

Images tell the story—a helicopter landing on the White
House lawn disgorging a disgraced president, a man who

Does not even have the courage or humanity to admit
Defeat—these times call for a different kind of strength,

Strength from our souls to turn out the vote as we never
Have before—perhaps the most important vote since before

Civil War times—people who work in the White House must
Wear full protective gear—working there is tantamount to

Attending a super-spreader event—have we ever lived through
A time with such a blatant disregard for human life, at least

Not since slavery ended—when can we ever agree on the value,
The importance, the dignity of every single human life?

Looking at John Singer Sargent's Painting of the Daughters of Edward Darley Boit

October light hangs crepuscular—rains are heavy today, clouds
Full, luminescent, opaque, last night rain came tumbling down,

Melting every orange leaf, yellows swirling autumnal, liminal,
Fall, letting evening come—so we have begun—gardens twirling

Like a carousel spinning at *Les Jardins du Luxembourg*—by the sea, it is
The turning of the seasons—COVID-19 has ceased our wanderings,

I am more restless than I would have believed possible, restless in the
Face of nothing, and yet everything—it is windy, windy where witches

Live, windy where bats fly, windy along the path to where we will not be turning
Back—four young girls stilled on the edge of consciousness.

October Wasps

A few Sundays ago, the wasps headed out of town, deserting the paper nest
They had constructed to last the summer, through Labor Day.

All summer long they buzzed around, but recently, they struck the
Set, tore it down, left it in tatters as they flew away—

Gray shards stripped down flapped in the wind, hanging off the corner
Of our house—a few stray wasps hung around—

Left behind by chance or choice, they hissed, angry at their desertion
Like birds left behind by their flock—the hurting must go on—

A lifetime's worth of hurt and betrayal, concentrated in a single summer—
now The wasps flee, the few stray ones ready to sting; they are not

Feeling the autumn calm, only the piercing pain of abandonment—they
Sting first you, then me, angry and free—

You on the shoulder, me on the finger when I pick up the wooden salad
Bowl leftover from a faraway time when I thought I chose

Once and it was forever—on this autumnal morning, you hand
Me ice and a bouquet of tangerine chrysanthemums.

Sewall Preserve

Let the light fall where it may—golden maples, birch, copper beech—
Stray goldenrod still growing far into October—
Piles of softened leaves beneath our feet—
Volunteers tending the land—pruning twigs, branches, limbs,
Now I understand the desire to steward
Earth—for those who come after us—
A stray orchid, a Lady Slipper blooming into fall—
Let the light fall where it may—as we
Fold into *Shavasana,* so we know
Where to begin, and also where to end—death
Seems less terrifying now I know where I will
Be resting—in a former asparagus field in a sleepy
Village I have known my whole life—from childhood,
Adolescence, young wife-hood, through becoming a
New mother, a first bereft daughter—and now,
As I raise my arms and let the world go free—here,
Here I can be, I no longer
Feel as though I have been locked out of the world—
Places where I have always wanted to be—
Let the light fall where it may—all through these sunny
October days.

Ledge

The work of mending is not easy—but unless it is work
We undertake of our free will,

The rocks will never be steady beneath our feet—we
Will only be setting ourselves up for a lifetime

Of unease, as the rocks can't shift beneath to support us—flint,
Ledge, granite, graphite, all the colors—

Each one rock gives us purchase—
It is easy to imagine tumbling into freefall—

But not when the skirt of rocks beneath us forms

To make our lives true, no one's foundation survives
Without cracks—but,

In irony, they can only stay extant, intact when they
Have cracks so they can bend like a San Francisco

Skyscraper swaying in an earthquake—in order to stand,
We need to know how to fall.

The Coral Reefs Are Dying

In my children's lifetimes, a quarter century, the coral reefs
Have lost half their mass, or more—and how, we ask, did this

Calamity happen? We are entering the age of Anthropocene—we
Have made our planet inhospitable for living—

And in this moment we have to choose—will it be earth, or us?
Or will we destroy both?

A high stakes game that, perhaps, we will be losing, but in
This moment as I look out on an autumnal morning, what

Matters is not how we got here, but what we will do now.

Americanski, Budapest, 1972

Deep inside a musty museum corridor, a woman grabs me—*Americanski,*
She whispers—she feels too close to me, her
Heavy, hot breath pours over me—

I am twelve, having just got my period in Budapest, an event
Which occasioned a red-cheeked bellhop bringing yards
Of cotton batting to our hotel room—

When the woman releases me, I spy a pair of blue eyeballs
Preserved in a case, staring back at me—my mother explains
This woman wants to be free, she believes America to be

A great country—almost fifty years later, I look out at these
United States and believe I have been witnessing
The country's descent into autocracy.

On Not Learning About Women in History

As I recall the way I learned American history, I realize
The women were invisible, unseen, standing behind Miles
Standish—

Men did things, women faded into the background to do
Whatever it is that men thought women did—

Perhaps that is why I wrote my eighth-grade research paper
On Mary Todd Lincoln because she was one of the few

Women whose name we learned—I wrote about how unseen
She was, alone in her depression, forced to come out of

The shadows of grief after she lost her son—and to behave,
As for the way I learned history, I wondered where the

Women were—

The day before our final exam, a boy in my
Class stole my notebook; there were no consequences,

As we like to say now.

Saqqara

In Egypt, archeologists have uncovered decorated coffins,
Some containing mummies, and statues in Saqqara—

Placed in the earth over two thousand years ago, they have stayed
Intact, decorated with gold, and jewels—

A glorious place for those who could afford it—glorious, the
Beauty of death venerated as celestial—a celebratory launching

To another world—and yet, and yet, for those who cannot afford
This voyage to the underworld, death comes by virus, bodies left

In morgue freezer trucks, not enough room at the inn quite
Literally, no good-byes can be said, sorrow fills the screens of

Loved ones, every American knows someone who has had COVID-19,
One third of Americans know someone who has died;

When will this knowing end?

Crescent Moon

In this day after a night of new moon,
We begin our yoga practicing lying on our
Left sides, our cooler sides, opening

Our hips—it is the opening that matters,
Opening to the shadow side of the moon

Which, of course, reflects the light
Of the sun—I am only a beginner here,

But I am starting to see the gifts of being
Able to move more freely through space—

To open our bodies to receive earth's
Pulsations—both warm and hot—

Filling us to the top with feeling, sensation,
Idealization—so we begin, we salute this

New crescent moon—arms raised
In salutation, not in hesitation.

The Asparagus Field

What passes for new in this colonial town dates
From at least the last century—

I have only spoken with the cemetery custodian
At times of distress—when my father died, then

My grandmother, then my mother, as must be true
For most of the conversations Tricia has—today

We speak on the phone with leisure—
She explains they've added some color,

Contour lately, mostly in the form of ornamental
Trees, to what used to be an asparagus field—

Deep into these months of unprecedented loss,
The virus sparing few, least of all what are now

Called the elderly, a category I just have entered—it
Seems only prudent to make some arrangements—

It's a bit like shopping for a house—she says it's a
No pressure sale—we agree to meet to inspect

The remaining open spaces.

The Bench, Musketaquid

December snow settles soft over these lands, this "grassy plain,"
Long settled, called, tilled, stilled, sewed, and hewn, by the
Musketaquid tribe who were here first—later, British settlers

Forced the tribe members from their land in an ugly, violent reclamation
Repeated across this country for centuries—later, these fields were planted with
Asparagus greening with the spring, with the settling of early graves—

As a boy, a cemetery director followed the backhoe to find arrowheads by
The dime—this Sleepy Hollow cemetery is filling fast—we stand by
A bench just beneath the flight path to Hanscom Air Force Base, jets

Fly by every few minutes, the current custodian jokes we could have
Our own flybys; a family has installed a set of chimes hanging from
An apple tree—here is where I will be when the time is right—

Beside a bench for sitting, a path for crossing, level open land for cross
Country skiers to pass by, for dogs to wander free.

Thanksgiving Is Cancelled This Year

Didn't you hear? Thanksgiving is cancelled this year—
Aerosols spread fast inside, without our masks—we
Can't very well eat turkey through a shield of cotton—

The worst possible thing we could do right would be
To squish together, young and old, around a table
In order to share a traditional feast: yams, potatoes,
Green beans—

It seems particularly cruel in this year of losing things—
Of losing funerals, good-byes, weddings, birthdays—
Not even to say the hundreds of thousands of
People—

That to gather for Thanksgiving would be about the cruelest
Thing we could do—to ask for a blessing—do you want
To kill someone? This would be a good day to stay
Away—

This is the way we need to live in order to stay alive
During these peculiar COVID times—

Goddess Pose

Towards the end of our practice we turn on our backs,
Spines pressed against our sticky mats, cool side
Underneath—

We bend our knees, straddling our bent legs out to the
Sides—with frog legs folded inside, pressed soles
One to other—

So as to feel the bottoms of our feet, skin pressed
To skin, a sensation we don't often recognize on our own—
Where our feet

Touch the ground, the two soles that connect us to earth
Where we stand our ground—

Let our legs fall where they may—close to earth—
The moment you were born, my solstice baby, they

Placed you on my chest until you turned blue; I
Recognized the fright in the room—the carnal fear
Of knowing you

Could slip away in that instant so soon after birth—
Until the crisis team arrived pushing their crash cart—

And began pounding on the bottoms of your
Feet until you started to scream.

Jupiter and Saturn, Aligned

This time, they align, an astronomical feat not to be repeated
For close to a century—

A third of a life, two thirds of a life, the years slip past, like
Sugar spooned into coffee—

The largeness of sky, the tininess of a grain of sugar, a riddle
To pass through a camel's eye—

On this day, my youngest son slipped out of me at 5:29 pm,
Eastern Standard Time—yet for months more, maybe years—

His cells stayed inside me, a recent discovery of seeing the
World in a grain of sand—

We do what we can to find the whole of who we are.

If There Were to Be a Memorial, What Would It Look Like?

Do you remember when the graphs began to rise higher?
Number, by number, by number nine months ago—long enough to grow
A human life—

Now, the first babies conceived in a pandemic are beginning to arrive—
How could we imagine the number of Americans who would have died

From the COVID-19? —As of this morning, over three hundred
And twenty-five thousand, though that number is only

Provisional—at the beginning, my youngest son told me he thought it would
Be bad, very bad—and he was not incorrect—I think of my daughter driving

Across Iowa to get her wedding dress fitted when news of the virus first broke—I
Imagine memorials to the Famine, what we also now know as

The Great Hunger, numbers too extraordinary to imagine—what memorials could
We erect now? In some places, chairs represent the number of lives lost—

Humans are terrible at understanding the dimensions of this catastrophe—
How can a human being be a chair? Even though tangible, the analogy appears
Faulty—

We have few points of reference to comprehend what has happened.

Late Afternoon December

Hills rise steep in front of me—if I leave the house by three, I can
Catch sunset from the crest—

Peaceful here now, the day after Christmas, just me and the dog—
I think of war, struggle, homelessness, bankruptcy, mortality—

Famine, we are all struggling to make our way through this
Diabolical year—the cold moon is almost full, but the

Missing slivers suggest just how much we've lost here on earth.

Winter Brook

Winter brook snakes beside a dirt road, first we thought its noise
Last spring was traffic, that its burbling was the thrum of cars roaring by,

But now, through drought and plenty we have realized its source in
Mountains above—today in snow it is full, robust, chunks of ice cling

To a crumbling stone wall, perhaps the remains of an early sawmill,
The dog prances, lifting on her hind legs to chase the burbling water.

Full Long Night's Moon

So, we have come to the last full moon this year
Of turmoil—our moon rises high, glaring through
A ring of hemlocks, this moon first named by

The Mohawks: Drift Clearing Moon, Frost Exploding
Trees Moon, Moon of the Popping Trees, Hoar Frost
Moon, Snow Moon, Ice Moon, Winter Making Moon,

Full Long Night's Moon, Long Night Moon, Wolf Moon;
The Pagans called it: Moon Before Yule—all these names, all
These moons, one and the same—

Noteworthy for being so high in the sky, staying
Above our horizons all night long, well into morning,
Crossing over our house, blue tinged light landing on squares

Of snow; we notice natural phenomenon more these days—
Called back upon our elemental natures—mortality
Edging ever closer to our lives.

Heather Corbally Bryant, PhD, is a Senior Lecturer in the Writing Program at Wellesley College. She has also taught at Harvard, the University of Michigan and the Pennsylvania State University where she has won awards for her teaching. She has written eleven books of poetry, a prize-winning academic book, *How Will the Heart Endure: Elizabeth Bowen and the Landscape of War,* and a work of creative nonfiction, *You Can't Wrap Fire in Paper*. Her poems have been nominated for a Pushcart Prize, the Massachusetts Book Award, and have won Honorable Mention in the Finishing Line Press Open Chapbook Competition.

www.ingramcontent.com/pod-product-compliance
Lightning Source LLC
Chambersburg PA
CBHW031125160426
43192CB00008B/1119
* 9 7 9 8 8 8 8 3 8 1 3 9 7 *